Tūnui | Comet

'*Tūnui | Comet* displays all the elegance, eloquence and craft one would expect from this Māori writer, who is one of the outstanding poets of his generation. This is a distinctive and rich collection about unity and location, using the compass of poetry to celebrate our archipelago of islands. Robert Sullivan has deftly fused the classicism of the European tradition with Māori animism and a new world wonder, even as he defamiliarises the ordinary.' — David Eggleton

'Sullivan's work is like a great camera: an eye in the sky that shows us all of who we are, then zooms right in to the specifics of the individual within the wider Māori identity. Under this Tūnui we are both the individual and the collective; the past and the future entwined in the poet's words. Sullivan is shapeshifter, time traveller, descendant and ancestor. We are all welcomed into the wharenui that this book has become.' — Ruby Solly

Tūnui | Comet

Robert Sullivan

AUCKLAND
UNIVERSITY
PRESS

First published 2022
Auckland University Press
University of Auckland
Private Bag 92019
Auckland 1142
New Zealand
www.aucklanduniversitypress.co.nz

ISBN 978 1 86940 969 2

A catalogue record for this book is available
from the National Library of New Zealand

Book design by Kalee Jackson

Cover art by Rae Joyce, 2021

This book was printed on FSC®
certified paper

Printed in China through Asia Pacific
Offset Group Ltd

Contents

Dedicated to my mother,
Maryann Teaumihi

Tētahi Waerea (Prayer of Protection)

Clouds are habits
over the seabed north and south
feeding mineral salts
spreading the eels' tails
and the eels' mouths.
Taniwha all of them.
Taniwha swimming to the Waikato,
taniwha in their weirs
in the Nōta (up home)
all the way to Tonga.

The eel in me is a taniwha
who protects, who swims, who speaks
in bubbles, who meows with whiskers
on fields, who slides in esses,
who babies, who plays with kina
softly, tentatively, between
anemones and shell-shuttling
crabbies lit in mild pink,
but as an eel I am dark.

The wannabe guitarist in me is a soloist
with a mike, on a stool, guitar
resting on my knee, song
pitched to my throat
sharing a Maisey Rika lyric.
Yeah, right.

Can't do the work for him, and I can't do the work for her.
Can share this. About Te Whare o tō mātou mātua tūpuna
and how our songs and voices in te reo Māori
lifted me with many pairs of arms
so I had wings again. Ka ora ka ora.
Thank you very much: ngā mihi nunui e te whānau.

Yes, I speak plainly, when I hear your voice,
bringing the unseen chains of a grandfather clock
and a Polynesian paddle into the conversation.
We stand tall before we play the clock out
past the reef toward Matariki. Clouds raise
their fists as seagulls and sparrows swoon
into the rainbow. It has been a long homecoming
and he has made the pieces one.

Māui's Mission

In the warmth of night I put feet to my plan: waited
for my brothers to sleep. They'd spent the day
sharpening their hooks, repairing the great net,
filling gourds with fresh water. They'd bundled
taro wrapped in leaves sitting below the cross seats.
The bundles and the net would cover me,
especially if I said the chant to slow my movement
and my breathing. The moon became brighter
like a huge fish eye as the chant hooked me.

I was holding my grandmother's hook so tightly
a little cut welled red between my closed knuckles.
'Good morning, brothers,' I called and they cussed
and moaned until the next chant took us a further hundred
miles and then another until my chanting made them gasp
as we settled on a patch of ocean black with fish.
They forgave me, not that it matters. I took the bloody hook
and said my business to the ocean. It worked.
The fish rose and our descent was secured.

Hello Great North Road

my old friend
I wonder how far north
you travel?
                    The road goes west
starting two doors up from The Dog's Bollix
ending at sunset.
                    So many sunsets
Facebook and Instagram couldn't contain them.
So many yellow lines, white stripes
there's hardly a Valiant left
to defy them.
                    Now the years overtake us.
Visits as a boy to Uncle Bruce and Aunty Lindy
in their K'Rd council flat
led me to the greatness of the great north
whipping its dusty tail up to the skyline
of Reinga.
                    Yet why do I see your
darkness as silence my friend?
You're a sleek black eel
pumping blood all the way to Karekare,
to Muriwai, to Bethells, to Piha,
and our vehicles surf the surges
back to K'Rd, back and forth, LOL,
rocking up our shock absorbers
and surfboards.
                    Keep bringing the waves
Great North Road. Keep saving
the whales! Keep the toheroas shining
tucked away from spades in sandy bolt-holes.
Smile in your cars and honk honk honk
on the Great North Road.

Kawe Reo / Voices Carry

Voice carries us from the foot of Rangipuke / Sky Hill / Albert Park
to the Wai Horotiu stream chuckling down Queen Street carrying
a hii-haa-hii story—from prams and seats with names and rhymes,
words from books and kitchen tables. Now we laugh again
in the St James stalls, in the bookstores, Seddon Tech, Patterson's
Stables, Odd Fellows Hall, art galleries and our great Library
gifted by our people who saved the words of our ancestors for one and all . . .

Decolonisation Wiki Entries

1. Family

Unfortunately, I won't be able to make this year's reunion
of the extended Wynyard family in the Bay of Islands. Our tupuna,
Hori Winiana, was the son of Robert Henry Wynyard and Anne Catherine
McDonnell. Wynyard commanded the 58th Regiment, bringing 200 troops
from Australia during the Northern Wars and was present
at Ruapekapeka Pā when it fell. He was born at Windsor.
His mother Jane Gladwin was a lady in waiting to Queen Charlotte, wife
of George III. His father William was a Lieutenant General. Hori, or George,
married our tupuna Iritana Pōmare. Their daughter Ihipera
married Te Kauhoa Harawene (or Sullivan) whose son was Turi
Sullivan who married Raiha Shepherd and their son was Massey
who married Matekino Ngakuru and their daughter was my mother, Maryann.

Iritana Pōmare's father was Pōmare II, the chief
of Ngāti Manu, who married Rangingangana, daughter
of the paramount chief of Ngāti Raukawa, Te Whatanui.
Iritana's brother was Hāre Pōmare, father of Albert Victor Pōmare,
godson of Queen Victoria, who joined the British navy and was lost at sea.

2. Ruapekapeka

I have visited once and seen a hilly field
from memory—hard to take the scene in
without props. There was a church service
and worshippers fled out beyond. Never
swarmed the bunkers and trenches.
Flicked between ancestor Wynyard
and our neighbouring great chief Kawiti.
I do not know the buried knives. We gathered
in this hill of ash, dead bees and pollen.
We left carvings in the earth and flowers there.

3. Treaty Training

The first communion here was in 1814. My grandmother
Matekino recited her bible in the dark with Granny Huru
and Granny Mohi. Tāwhirimātea's tongue stretched ahead
while Tū turned his the other way. 'We are the champions
of the world' sang Freddy Mercury at Live Aid.
I take these crumbs and eat them.
Train myself to load the dishwasher
and empty it. When my training is complete
I will be ready to learn about the Treaty.

A.O.U.

A Ahakoa he iti, he mihi ki Te Ahi Kā o Ihumātao. Pai mārire ki a koutou katoa.	Although it is brief, a mihi to the home fires of Ihumātao. Peace and blessings to you all.
O Ōna tāngata whenua ōna manaakitanga ki a mātou o Tāmaki Herenga Waka.	Its peoples of the land its mana enhancing care for us of Tāmaki that binds many canoes.
U Utaina mai te waka. I rere a Uenuku ki runga ake o Puketutu. Te ātaahua, te mamae, me te tapu.	Load up the canoe. Uenuku (the rainbow) flew above Puketutu Island. The beauty, the pain, and the sacred.

Feathers

I wake up, trousers spattered
in mud, vomit, someone's blood
Leave Parihaka for my bell tent
to tidy up

Back in the bell tents we sing
singing the regimental colours
singing the family songs
we're a little band of brothers
marching hundreds strong

Second Feather
I'm a feather in flight
I'm a feather on a drum
I'm a feather from the sky

Te Puapua
Raukura
E tū

E rere wai
Poi in Flight
      loft
          slide
puff
    fly
        hip hip
tip
   and slide
tip and glide
flip pip
    hā hā
hī
the third feather

Whiteness
of the mountain
the ploughs
and feathers
the children's
singing
witness

Kōwhai

1.

We walked through the pine forest this late morning
with its tree ferns (ponga), mānuka, cabbage trees (tī rākau),
and pulled a stump out so that folks wouldn't stub
themselves in the dark. It was sunny for once
and a little warm which was a relief after the rain
and southerlies from icier parts had driven in frosts,
allowing us to create dewy walking trails on the field
and cricket pitch leading us into the forest
to see how our trails met and diverted and met.

2.

The previous week I had seen a kingfisher
sitting in my front yard (well it isn't my front
lawn, I'm renting here), just as I was signing
an 80th birthday card which was very special
as I knew it was a sign too. We went to the party
which was massive, for a beloved kuia
of both Ngāti Hau and Ngāti Whātua who has led
our people in the city for many decades. This kuia
knew my grandmother. She is a māreikura, a noble
taonga of all the people. Happy birthday Whaea Awa.

Ah

With Cook's new things
we built spacious homes
made from fallen shingles
and nīkau leaves,
with branches that had
already landed
on moss.
We learned to see
with spectacles,
and used our own
medicines in vials,
and ointments,
and shared them
with the sailing ships
that came to buy
our medicines,
carvings, cloaks
and food.
The trees
got to live.
The beaches
lined the coasts
as they always had,
white sand, gold sand,
black sand
and shells.

Cooking with Gas

(for Rachel)

After the first expedition I went home to Mrs Cook
and our lovely little Stepney home. I could have waited.
They'd given me a Greenwich pension.
I could have dined out with rear admirals
and royals. But it was the press made me do it.
They kept talking me up. By George,
I had to go out there again, and a third time too
like a Hollywood mogul. What if
I had turned the ships around,
sailed back to Deptford or Whitby,
dropped the RN and the FRS?
Handed it over to Banks
and his orchestra like he wanted?
Or what if I stayed in Aotearoa
and shared our science,
our medical knowledge,
our carpentry and animal husbandry,
our love of books
and conservation values?
What if we had gained the friendship,
love and trust of the Natives,
and returned that equally
at the time, not needing
to constantly gaslight
and to make amends?

Reading List

I've been reading about topsails and studding sails,
broken topmasts and barnacles, winds that come
from the south or the west, soundings, latitude,
longitude and compass roses, sextants and quadrants,
travel clocks and scurvy, sauerkraut and lemon juice,
Newfoundland and a schooner from Massachusetts,
a man's boyhood in Marton-in-Cleveland,
his learning in the Postgate School at Ayton,
his apprenticeship as a shop assistant in Staithes,
and his later apprenticeship at Whitby
which we visited fleetingly.

I never wrote about his boyhood before.

i wasn't a poet for writing placenames

i was a foreman's son who expanded
the admirals' imperio cogito
never-setting horizons ergo sum
thanks to sharp clocks
and well-scribed logs
going to australis incognita
tahiti or the antarctic
skipping and bobbing in a coal scuttle
with telescopes
and extra credit for a scurvy cure
a pension for mrs cook
royal navy posts for the boys
opera glasses and poetry
engraved tomes
a sci-fi series
and perseverance
for repairing our endeavour
from a reef when we should
have mended the coral . . .
      dance's oil painting stitched me
in a wig with my dress uniform
gold buttoned in some map room
pointing at australia
yet i could've been
dressed for fifty shades of grey
with my fine curls a cut above
bloody rum barrels and other
bligh whipping tales about
my severed burial at sea.

Old Government House

I want to wrap Old Government House
like Christo and Jean-Claude
I want to wrap Old Govt House
in pages of the Treaty
I want to wrap OGH
in lavalavas
I want to wrap OGH
in fine feather cloaks
I want to wrap OGH
in tartans
I want to wrap OGH
in parachute silk in balloon rubber
I want to wrap OGH
in illuminated vellum
I want to wrap OGH
in four enormous kanji blankets
for the north wind
for the south east and west winds
I want to rap its doors and say open sesame
so I did

pome

I'm writing this in Ōamaru
knowing that Hone will have a barbecue at his place
in Kaka Point about two hours from here on Sunday.
It's great his crib has been restored. It'd be brill
to see Tangaroa's tonsils in person
but I want my family to be safe
from the virus. To Hone's whānau
tēnā koutou katoa. Ka nui te hari koa
ki te mōhio te oranga o tana whare.

Our Pōwhiri for the International Students

At the marae today we hosted about 150 visitors from India and the Pacific.
We spoke about our house being the kete that contains the knowledge
of love and peace. How our marae is named after the baskets
of knowledge. That they are most welcome. I led the prayer.
Then another team member gave the first mihi. They had two
speakers from their side. Then I closed our speeches
and invited the front row to hongi, while pointing to my nose
for each visitor to press their nose to rather than bumping foreheads.

Our visitors loved the welcome as we welcomed them to our country
and we wanted them to feel that they belonged, that it was their new home.
Nau mai rā.

The Declaration of Independence

(for Moana Jackson)

in Aotearoa was not one. It was an assertion of mana
by our rangatira—not a mention of independence
as we were already there. Why is this viewpoint
not widely shared? Why are we talked to about
the Treaty when it is Te Tiriti that was signed by us
and He Wakaputanga spells it out so very clearly
in black and white with our nose moko
as signatures—can you get any closer?

He Wakaputanga

Nō roto o Aotearoa. Ka whakaputa i ngā reo,
i ngā mana o Ngāi Rangatira o te motu. Kāore e kī
i ngā kupu tūhāhā. Nā te aha i kore ai e pānui i tēnei
tirohanga. Kei hea te pai ki te kōrero mō The Treaty;
koia nei Te Tiriti i hainatia e mātou, kua mārama i ngā
hainatanga o ngā ngū moko—ka whakatata rawa ake
i te hā rangatira. Ka whakaputa i te mana motuhake.

Sunday

I mow the grass
and leave a strip
for birds and insects
to feed on
full of flowers
while the neighbours mulch theirs
to the thinnest green

A little

When the developers fit
      the last daisy chain
      into the last plastic
      balcony tub
      for potted colour
      in the estate agent's window

When the prices stop rising
      as high as apartments
      riding the K'Rd ridge
      all the way to Ponsonby
      and Grey Lynn
      cranes swinging

When the dark side of the moon
      features the lunar goddess
      Chang'e
      and these pen strokes
      turn vertical and across
      to indicate the importance of people

When the oceans of the moons of Jupiter
      and Saturn move like ours
      with songs fins and eyes alight
      and ears to gauge
      through liquid and crystal
      night

Only then will I buy

Petal

The Crane's-Bill you held to me to exercise
my hand has disappeared into yesterday
like the tip of the Cabbage Tree burnt off
by a sun that has no forest to soothe it.

Dream

I woke with the birds.
We were on a bus somewhere in England,
a double-decker red one and the driver
turned up an arterial which had turned to grass.
He turned us around and took us commuters
in the reverse direction. We were
working our way through the contents
of my soft gym bag which was filled with beads,
shiny coins, and we'd piled them up on the bus floor
so a young boy with his parents sitting opposite us
dived into them before I could scoop them back.

I had asked the bus driver if he could let a passenger know
that they might miss their bus stop now that
we had changed direction, but he instead quoted
from a lengthy passage of *Hamlet*.

Ruia

These ripples circling outward and outward in the first instance
belong in the language of our ancestors, ruia ruia tahia tahia
as the bar-tailed godwits fly from the Manukau to Alaska

and we step into the soil of the harbour floor.
Each step quickly fills on the lifting squelch
as the land from the hillsides covers our old sandy shores.

We can repair this I know. Patiently and with care
bring back the sandy beaches, end the oil draining
into inlets, the plastic, the chemicals, and endless rubbish

by thinking a little harder with our hearts soaring up
with the kūaka, and singing like them, in squeaks
rather than arias, so we travel further.

Untitled

I am left alone in this house
with its bush track
where tūī sing from their puku
but all I hear are owls
telling me to tangi
but my puku holds on
my ngākau pleads
like a black tīwakawaka
sitting on a little tree

He Toa Takitini

I began writing this poem in te reo English to be understood;
it's the language I was brought up speaking, despite
my mother's parents both being fluent speakers of Māori.
In time I will write in Māori, enough to carry poems into
the whakaaro Māori i ngā āhuatanga katoa o tōna tikanga
i rō o āku tuhituhinga. These kupu buds flutter on twigs
in the roar of English, and sometimes I am reminded by non-speakers
not to use this language because it cannot be understood by non-speakers
which perpetuates a cycle of disuse. It's quite an interesting problem.
Tōku raru. E ai ki te reo rangatira, he rākau hei whakamaru i te iwi,
hei whakarākei i ngā oranga o te tangata. E pēhi tonu ana
nā te haukino o te wā engari ka tipu, ka hua ngā purapura
hei whakarauora tō tātou reo mō ngā tāngata katoa
ahakoa nō hea ahakoa ko wai.

Te Whitianga a Kupe

1.

Last week we celebrated the arrival of the waka hourua of Kupe
Matawhaorua about 1100 years ago and HMB *Endeavour* in 1769
of then Lieutenant James Cook.
Kupe's wife Hine Te Aparangi,
according to Ngāti Hei, named the islands Aotearoa
which refers to the Māori name for Great Barrier Island,
Aotea, with the main landmass of the Coromandel
marked by its high peaks observed by her as the longer,
'roa' of Aotearoa. When they landed, Kupe named the first landing
or crossing, Te Whitianga a Kupe.*
                              When Cook arrived
for twelve days in November 1769, he named
Te Whanganui o Hei Mercury Bay. They were there
to see the Transit of Mercury on November 9
so that the astronomer Charles Green could work out
the longitude of Terra Australis Incognita.
The crew gave other names such as the Aldermen Islands
for their high rock needles like a court.

*John Steele and Richard Gates, *When Toawaka Met Cook: Stories of Whanganui o Hei –
Mercury Bay*, Mercury Bay Trust, Whitianga, 2019.

2. Tuia

Whakarongo ake ki te tangi a te mātui
tui, tui tui tuia.

On the Tuia Stage in Whitianga there were rock groups,
poets and a choir. The tangata whenua, Ngāti Hei,
graced the stage with whaikōrero and waiata tawhito.
It was humbling to listen to their kaumātua
who spoke of the importance of harmony
between us, Māori and Pākehā, represented
by this celebration of waka and the *Endeavour*.

3. Waka Tipa

I moved between the tents, across the road to the harbour
where three waka moored. I came aboard the waka hourua, Haunui,
led by Hoturoa Barclay-Kerr, the great star navigator and rangatira.
I spoke with some of his crew, including the captain
of Fa'afaite, the Tahitian waka tipa, which surfed huge waves
at 22 knots to arrive in time for the celebrations
from Tahiti. I then walked down the pier to their waka
and doubled my exposure to these taonga in person.

4. Stardome

I learnt about the star compass and knot making
with some other tourists who were from
the crew of the *Endeavour* replica moored
off Wharekaho. They talked to the guide
about the knots they used and tried to show us.
I couldn't even remember the knots' names
let alone tie them. It was always a problem
for me in scouts. That's right, they talked about reef
knots, and there was this huge knot made from
three loops of rope. Then we lay next to each other
in the stardome tent looking at the video
of the waka sailing, and then the stars projected
onto the tent roof. I spotted matariki
because there were nine points of light!

5. Star Waka

What was beautiful is that my friend the artist
Maureen Lander invited me to Whitianga
through her friends—artist Chris Charteris
and weaver Lizzy Leckie. Chris made the frame
for the waka and then members of the community,
mainly children, made stars from ice-cream sticks,
bracken, and wool, with feathers on the waka.
They hung some of the stars from the tent ceiling
and many were in a pool of stars below the waka.
The group of weavers Maureen leads are called
Ngā Turuturu o te Tara, a Coromandel name.

6. Following Up

It turns out that some of the Tahitians
are staying in the two other marae in Ōtara,
Ngāti Ōtara and Whaiora Marae. They're here
for the Tuia celebrations in Auckland.
This time the *Endeavour* moored in the port
because there's deep water. I've parked
Star Waka just off Rangitoto
to catch the starlight lining the mountain's
silhouette when looking away from the city.

7. Āraiteuru

Soon the Star Waka will move our blended rōpū
to Ōamaru not far from where the tūpuna waka
Āraiteuru landed at Moeraki. We've bought a home
close to my Dad's Ngāi Tahu side. I'll go and represent
my Nana Sarah at two of our marae, Puketeraki,
and Ōtākou, with tremendous pride.

8. H. G. Wells

If only I could move forward ten years
in a time machine, bring the family with me,
enjoying the government's successful
reshaping of the education sector
where education is strongly linked
to wellbeing outcomes for all.

9. Standing Up

This past autumn has been blustery
with the winds of further change
sweeping through all the polytechs
and Industry Training Organisations
waiting for April 1
to be governed by a single board.
It's an intergenerational change
invoking the Moorish Wars
and the defence of Castile
by a corpse on a horse,
the splendidly suited
Cid, Rodrigo of Vivar,
set in a saddle
'with a board between
its shoulders'* by his servant
Gil Diaz. His steed Babieca
stands resolute before the people
who struggle on.

*From W. S. Merwin (trans.), *The Poem of the Cid*,
J. M. Dent & Sons, London, 1959.

10. Mauri

The Fa'afaite carried mauri stones
from its travels including stone from Taputapuātea,
and obsidian from Tūhua (Mayor Island).
I touched them with my hands.

11. Listing

I compiled an inventory of items for Cook's second voyage
from Beaglehole's *The Life of Captain James Cook*,
but I misplaced it. I looked for it in my subconscious.
There was greed, curiosity, lasciviousness, cruelty,
inferiority complexes, jealousy, claims to cure scurvy,
a big ego, hunger for fish and chips, plus an ignorance
of what it meant setting out without blue blood.
Then I began looking in my desk for the list.

12. When We Left in the Waka

we left the turtles behind
great honu who followed
the moon and stars too
but we had it in our heads
that we were the stars
and so we left the turtles
their eggs in the beaches
for our cold raw selves

13. Thousand-Faced Waka

a myriad choral voices
in the singing of the mōteatea,
the Mahabharata, the Kumulipo,
the oceanic and earthly spires
on the thousand thousand journeys
roaming the jagged ribs
of singers swimming
the ocean's billion
billion ashes
this waka weaves
stories of bazaars
and pig husbandry
duetted by sailors
who studded
the Araby
and came
out of Pele's
mouth

14. Cookies

A cup of tea
a picture of the *Endeavour*
replica on my phone
from the beach
on my way back
and the upload
to our Five Eyes
partners
confirming
I was there

Homage to Alistair

My soul will take
the Interislander
because it can carry
my bags, a van
and a furniture trailer
with fifty years' worth
of boxes.

My soul will take
the Interislander
because it's grounded.
Rubber on road
keeps one safe
from lightning
and it's a roll-on roll-off

ferry with a café
and deck to see
the Southern Alps
plus the Picton end
has a park bench
where I sat in Auntie's
cardy and didn't care.

My soul will take
the Interislander
as if it's a frigate bird
over Tongareva
or the twin engine
that touches down
on blue moons like

a dark lord seeking
his authentic indigenous voice
among the faraway hills
of Kāpiti and Troy.

Homage to Te Whatanui

Te Ariki nō roto o Ngāti Raukawa

I sense the talk
from the centre of the island
to return to Maungatautari

but I will not be made
the subject of scraping cicadas,
turned into a dog

like Irawaru by that impious
Māui, jealous of his sister's
love beyond the pull

of his old homeland,
drawn out by Hina's
skill with the tides.

I will stay here
and wānanga with our people
in the Horowhenua.

I have sent my daughter
north where the sky
bathes the most red,

Te Rangingangana. Rātou ki a rātou
te hunga mate, mātou ki a mātou
te hunga ora, tēnā tātou katoa.

Rongo kōrero au.

Decolonising the Coastline

I'd been down at Moeraki attempting to see the same
midges and kelp as Keri Hulme who had written
The Silences Between: Moeraki Conversations yet
instead I sat in the rental on the edge of the highway
at Waikouaiti. In my defence I did get out and walked
down the grassy bank over stones onto the sand. There
was a shag there like the ones on the skeletal pier
at Ōamaru. I'd also seen a fur seal at Moeraki
which wasn't moving, just two hundred feet
from the throng of tourists gathered around
the boulders which looked like biological
shape toys, too round to be eggs, hexagonal
lines spread on the surface waiting for the pieces.
I carefully did not photograph the seal
so as not to draw attention to us.
The couple in the SUV next to me drove off.
That's when I started walking on the sand,
trying to remember Hulme's place names.

Rock Art

The sign said Maori Rock Drawings
so no wonder the mature male cyclist
said to the group of women
what makes the pigeons Māori?
He cackled at his own joke.
I allowed it to ruin my drive
to Ōmarama—I nearly turned
around to talk to him,
but then allowed the land,
the other limestone cliffs
with our tūpuna art,
our taonga tuku iho,
remind me what was what
and who was who.

Conservation

The blue penguins have little wooden boxes
placed in mounds near the tourist stadiums.
I went to watch them coming home
from their ocean commute—waddling in single file,
pairs and clusters up to their enclosed area
where we'd watch them slide or fall down the mounds
squawking to each other. I was in the cheap seats
so it only cost me $35 for a single ticket.
I wish I was in the expensive seats
cause the penguins would waddle right by them.

Steam

You need great literacy and numeracy
to have a career in Steam subjects. This town
has a lot of Victorian architecture—
old grain silos, railway sheds, public
buildings with Graeco-Roman columns—
so they've named it the Steampunk Capital.
I like the arching waterfront walkway
that takes you to the penguins,
and look forward to when I throw a kayak
into the bay with its small yachts
and power boats. I haven't counted.

Te Tāhuhu Nui

1.

Ka kī atu a Kupe, 'Purutia iho tō wheke! E haere ana ngā waka āpōpō ki te hī ika.'
Kupe said, 'Restrain your octopus! The canoes are going fishing tomorrow.'

Thirteen tupuna lines of the hapū have gathered—at Te Kāretu, and now here
at Ngā Kete Wānanga Marae to kōrero about the Treaty claim. Our claims

are many. We discuss the wellbeing of other hapū, our whanaunga.
Matua Arapeta talks to us about the history of our people, our origins,

right up until the destruction of Ōtuihu by the British. Cousin Phoebe
takes us through the claims process and the entities we will establish

post-settlement. Arapeta asks for comment throughout the house, and asks
patiently again and again if anyone wishes to speak. Then after a while,

he asks us for our support. We all say yes. Not one voice opposed.
We all say āe! So our hapū is the first to stand up on our own.

2.

Ka hoki a Kupe ki te iwi, ka mea atu, 'Mahia taku waka kia pai!'
Kupe returned to the tribe and said, 'Prepare my canoe!'

As we went around the whare, Te Kete Uruuru Matua, the kete
holding the knowledge of love and peace, in response to the kōrero

from Matua Arapeta and Cousin Phoebe, our kuia Aunty Bessie spoke.
She spoke of our Aunty Judy who prepared the way for this time

whose strength created our kōhanga reo, and the kura, and her moko
fluent in te reo Māori me ōna tikanga. Aunty Judy was on the Board

of St Stephens, and was a Queen Victoria graduate, whose father
Great Uncle Hone Hapa was my grandad's oldest brother and was killed

with his other brother, Great Uncle Johnson, in North Africa
during the War. Aunty Judy and her daughters looked after

our Nanny Ina who didn't have children of her own
in her pensioner's flat in Kawakawa so she had dignity

at the end of her days and knew the love, and respect
of the whānau together in Kāretu where she was born.

Hoki wairua mai, e okioki mai ki waenganui i te whānau.
The journey has been hard and remains so except for our love.

3.

Ka kī atu a Kupe ki tana wahine, 'Hoake ki runga i te waka kia kotahi ai tō
   tāua mate!'
Kupe said to his wife, 'Go onto the canoe so that we two shall die together!'

Gently we spoke. Talked about our families, introducing siblings and children,
those of us who live at Kāretu and those who don't. The whānau

at home were at pains to tell us they regarded us all as one and that
it was the government who required them to hold hui in the tāone

away from Kāretu to pānui the settlement process and our position.
Some spoke about our members of parliament and government ministers

who are Ngāti Manu and how we'd love to see them at these gatherings
but unfortunately they'd be seen as conflicts of interest

so they can't come. That might be unfair though as I'm reporting this
second-hand. You know how Rousseau said we're all in chains?
   Ka mōhio ahau.

No worries my whanaunga. We'll all be together after this dust
has died down. We'll be singing along side by side in our urupā.

4.

Ka karanga a Kupe, 'Makaia ngā tahā nā ki te upoko o te wheke!'
Kupe called, 'Throw these calabashes onto the head of the octopus!'

We would have been part of the hapū collective arranged by the iwi
clustered at Taumārere near the maunga of Rākaumangamanga,

one of the mountain pillars of the sacred house of Ngāpuhi.
We decided to stand as Ngāti Manu to be heard

speaking for ourselves while remaining respectful and supportive
of other hapū who we connect and tie to, and honour them

by being pono and tika. Another part of our claim
is mana wāhine and recognising that our female tūpuna

were rangatira and deserved to be dealt with on an equal basis
as our male tūpuna by the government. Our leaders

worked together. So, we are only putting women
forward for the Waitangi National Trust.

5.

I've misplaced my book of *Selected Readings in Māori* compiled
by Professor Biggs and Professor Hōhepa so I don't have a quote

from our tupuna Kupe's travels in Aotearoa. It's a faded yellow
hardback with a two-centimetre-thick spine. I started looking

in Sisson, Wi Hongi and Hōhepa's *Ngā Pūriri o Taiamai* but
decided against it as it would mix the wairua. Instead I'll look

into my heart and my grandmother's village
of Omanaia, near the birthplace of the Ngāpuhi people,

and set my sights on the sands of Ōmāpere
near the houses of knowledge of our competing priests

who landed the whale that gave the Hokianga
its distinctively spiritual name, Hokianga that exhausts

prayers. Our grandmother rests in the Omanaia cemetery
with all the nannies we never knew because

she passed away when our mum was still a girl.
We have some of our tūpuna's papers in Auckland Museum

on her side of the whānau which tell the beginning
of Ngāpuhi like a comet filling the sky.

6.

I'd written 'Decolonisation Wiki Entries'
because it reminded me of buses in Honolulu

at the airport and Waikiki. The open-air buses
aren't like decolonisation though. Decolonisation

is not worrying about cultural identity,
and not translating and not having to explain

things a family and hapū do such as wānanga
because the wānanga is the explanation

or learning mōteatea by our ancestors,
or prophesies of our spiritual tūpuna, or sadness

at the fighting on the other side. These
decolonisations make up life.

7. Whakarongo mai

Forgive my ignorance about some of our whakapapa.
I've made mistakes like who was our first Sullivan tupuna:

Captain Charles William Baldwin Sullivan, or William
Harken Sullivan? It's confusing. You can look it up

on ancestry.com to see this divergence. Members of the family
remain unsure about this. Someone knows bits about these

tūpuna, and someone else knows about others. Knitting
together all the knowledge requires wānanga in the marae

and a very good memory and whanaunga who remain
fascinated by this. Printed words tend to stick to the page

and last longer than the knowledgeable kōrero
of our kaumātua and kuia. But for those

who made the effort to listen to the pakeke
they know their spoken truth and mana.

By the way I found a potter, Michael Sullivan,
who passed away at Pōmare's pā in the early 1830s!

8.

Yet I know the first Sullivan with our Māori surname, Harawene,
was our tupuna Hikuwai who was born around 1825. His father was either

Charles or William or maybe Michael. Hikuwai married Mereana Kawhena,
from the Tainui waka. Her mother was a Kingi. Their son was Te Kauhoa
  who married

our Ngāti Manu tupuna, Ihipera Winiana, whose parents were Hori Winiana
and Iritana Pōmare whose parents were Rangingangana and Whetoi Pōmare.

Hori's (George's) parents were Robert Henry Wynyard and Anne Catherine
  (nee McDonnell).
The McDonnells were Highlanders from Aberchalder. Their forebears joined
  forces

with the Jacobite army, later becoming officers in the British military
serving all over the world. I didn't know that before writing this.

Ka Ruku

Ka rere atu ki te kanohi taumata
o te pari, ki ngā kupu tapu o reira,
ki ngā kupu noa hoki
o tana kauae raro.

Ka parirau te ngākau nui
o te kōhungahunga, arā,
ko Rūaumoko—ka mirimiri au
i tana Māmā, ā, ka hikoi ki te pae.

Whakarongo e hoa mā ki te whaitiri
o te ao rino. I kite mātou i te hihiko
o ngā waea. Kua tā ake rātou
i te mata o te whenua—ngā haehae

o te ao hou. Ka tae mātou ki te pae.
Ka kite mātou i te tōnga o te rā.
Ka rongo i te makariri, engari,
ka tiaho ake i ngā whetū wātea.

Kei te ora tonu hoki mātou.
Kei te noho tonu i te whenua.
Ka taea ētahi o mātou te hiki
i ngā whatu ki te rangi. Ka taea.

Karakia Whakakapi

I pā ahau ki a Papatūānuku
te whaea o te ao
ka tukua aku ringa ki Ranginui kei runga
te matua o te kikorangi
ā, papaki rawa iho te tau o taku ate
horomia iho i rō i te ngākau
ki te ipu wai roha
e pupuri ana i ngā tumomo kōhatu:
te mea tūpono,
te āwangawanga,
te mokemoketanga,
te takinga,
kia kaha ai koe, roha ngā parirau
o te manawanui
ā, whakarērea nei te mihi
karangatia hī ki te whenua
karangatia hā ki te rangi
ka homai, ka hoatu ngā tāngata
mā roto i ēnei uaua
ōrite ki te rauiti uaua
o te raupua e mānu ana
ki roto i tērā ipu wai
ngā mihi ki a koe e te tuakana,
ngā mihi ki a koe e te tuahine,
me hōngi harirū tātou,
me pōrutu i ā tātou hoe
me whakahā rawa iho
me inu i te wai aroha
ka karanga tonu tātou i te whakamihi
ka tū i te hui nei kei runga i te whenua toitū
wirihia tonutia ngā ringa o te tira haukainga e.

Comet

I'm writing a comet
from my tupuna, Papahurihia,
which from the earth
looks like a long tail
this ancestor whose headstone
turned around overnight

we are the only direct ones
Nanny Ipu's and Nanny Mate's
children and mokopuna
from the prophet
who said the prayers
for Hone Heke

numbers and stars
kōrero about the comet
family lineages
land deeds
and lists
in our tupuna's papers

repetitions of sunrises
and sunsets
so many we couldn't
keep track
of all the papers
held by the Nākahi

the so-called cult
of followers

named after the serpent
on Moses' staff
a serpent that reminds me
of a Ngāpuhi taniwha eel
that turns a grave
into a light

Acknowledgements

Poems have appeared in the following publications: *The Canary,
Cordite Poetry Review, The Galway Review, Landfall,* NZ Poetry Shelf, *Poetry,
Poetry New Zealand, Shenandoah, takahē.*

'Kawe Reo / Voices Carry' is installed on the front steps of Auckland Central
City Library.

'A.O.U.' was part of Michel Tuffery's exhibition, *Polyfonts.*

'Feathers' is one of the lyrics I wrote for *Witnessing Parihaka,* a composition
by Stephen Matthews. It was performed by Stuart Devenie, Te Kohe Tuhaka
and the Auckland Philharmonia Orchestra in 2011 at the Aotea Centre.

'Te Tāhuhu Nui' includes Kupe quotes taken from Bruce Biggs,
He Whiriwhiringa: Selected Readings in Māori, Auckland University Press,
Auckland, 1998.

'Karakia Whakakapi' is my translation of the poem 'Karakia' (for Bruce
Stewart) which was published in *Piki ake!* Thanks to Dr Wahineata
Smith, Luana Tehira, Dr Rapata Wiri and Melba Pakinga for feedback
and suggestions on its translation. Thanks also to Rapata and Melba for
suggestions for the other poems in te reo Māori. Any errors are my own.

Many thanks to Sam Elworthy and the wonderful team at AUP for
supporting this publication.

Robert Sullivan is the author of a number of books of poetry including *Star Waka* (Auckland University Press, 1999), which has gone through multiple reprints, a graphic novel and a prize-winning book of Māori legends for children. He co-edited, with Albert Wendt and Reina Whaitiri, the anthologies of Polynesian poetry in English, *Whetu Moana* and *Mauri Ola*, and an anthology of Māori poetry with Whaitiri, *Puna Wai Kōrero*. He has taught at the University of Hawai'i at Mānoa and Manukau Institute of Technology, and is currently Māori Dean at Waitaki Boys' High School. Robert belongs to the iwi Ngāpuhi Nui Tonu and Kāi Tahu.